KT-420-327

Big Machines Drive!

Catherine Veitch

Raintree is an imprint of Capstone Global Library Limited, a company incorporated in England and Wales having its registered office at 7 Pilgrim Street, London, EC4V 6LB – Registered company number: 6695582

www.raintreepublishers.co.uk
myorders@raintreepublishers.co.uk

Edited by Helen Cox Cannons and Kathryn Clay
Designed by Tim Bond and Peggie Carley
Picture research by Mica Brancic and Tracy Cummins
Production by Helen McCreath
Originated by Capstone Global Library Ltd
Printed and bound in China by Leo Paper Group

ISBN 978 1 406 28455 3
18 17 16 15
10 9 8 7 6 5 4 3 2

British Library Cataloguing in Publication Data
A full catalogue record for this book is available from the British Library.

Acknowledgements
We would like to thank the following for permission to reproduce photographs:

Alamy: ©dpa picture alliance archive, 19, ©Natrow Images, 14, 15, 22c; Corbis: Demotix/© Stephen Barnes, 12, 13; Getty Images: E+/BanksPhotos, 8, 9, front cover, VOLKER HARTMANN/AFP, 18; Liebherr: 16, 17, 22d; NASA: 4, 5, 22b, back cover; Newscom: EPA/BERND WEISSBROD, 20; Rex Features: David Bagnall, 10, 11; Shutterstock: justasc, 21; SuperStock: Tips Images, 6, 7, 22a, back cover.

Every effort has been made to contact copyright holders of material reproduced in this book. Any omissions will be rectified in subsequent printings if notice is given to the publisher.

All the Internet addresses (URLs) given in this book were valid at the time of going to press. However, due to the dynamic nature of the Internet, some addresses may have changed, or sites may have changed or ceased to exist since publication. While the author and publisher regret any inconvenience this may cause readers, no responsibility for any such changes can be accepted by either the author or the publisher.

Contents

Some words are shown in bold, **like this.** You can find out what they mean by looking in the glossary.

Crawler transporters

A crawler transporter carries
rockets to the launch pad.
The crawler lowers its sides
and rolls under a rocket
to lift it.

With its heavy load,
the crawler travels only
1.6 kilometres (1 mile)
per hour.

Road trains

The longest trucks in the world are called road trains. Instead of pulling just one **trailer**, these giant trucks pull three or more.

Giant tractors

These are not your average tractors. Giant tractors have eight tyres with thick **grooves**. The tractors weigh 10 times more than a car.

cab

Farmers climb a ladder to get into this **cab.**

Big Super **Mighty**
Size

groove

Combine harvesters

Farmers use combine harvesters to separate seeds from the rest of the plant.

The Lexion 590R is one of the world's largest combine harvesters. Every minute the combine **harvests** 80 **bushels** of corn.

Monster trucks

Huge tyres turn these vehicles into monster trucks. Drivers show off for big crowds during competitions.

Strong bars inside the driver's cab protect the driver if the truck rolls over.

Super truck

Meet one of the largest trucks in the world. The Terex Titan can carry two buses at once!

This truck is no longer on the road. It is now a **tourist** attraction in Canada.

Mobile cranes

The Liebherr Company built the world's strongest and tallest crane. It can be driven to where it's needed.

boom

A long **boom** reaches high into the air.

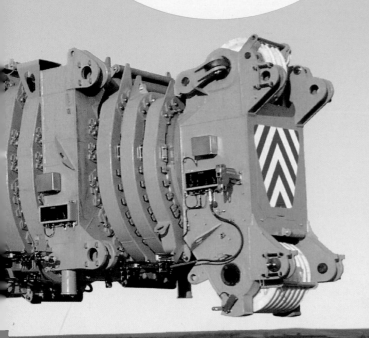

Big Super **Mighty**

Size

Motorcycles

The Gunbus 410 is one of the largest motorcycles in the world. It is 3.4 metres (11 feet) long.

Dream Big is a record-breaking bike. It took Greg Dunham three years to build this mega motorcycle.

Sizing things up

Dream Big Motorcycle

Engine...............	500 horsepower
Height...............	3.4 metres (11.3 feet)
Weight..............	2.6 metric tons (2.9 tons)
Tyres...............	188 centimetres (74 inches)

Grave Digger Monster Truck

Engine................	up to 1,700 horsepower
Weight	4.5 metric tons (5 tons)
Tyres................	168 centimetres (66 inches)

Quiz

How much of a Machine Mega-Brain are you?
Can you match each machine name to its correct photo?

**crawler transporter • Terex Titan
mobile crane • road train**

1

2

3

4

Check the answers on the opposite page
to see if you got all four correct.

Glossary

boom a mechanical arm

bushel a unit of measurement used to measure amounts of corn

cab an area for a driver to sit in a large truck or machine

groove a long, narrow channel cut into a surface

harvest to gather crops, such as corn or wheat

tourist a person who travels and visits places for fun or adventure

trailer the part of a semitruck where goods are loaded and carried

Quiz answers:
1. road train 2. crawler transporter
3. Terex Titan 4. mobile crane

23

Find out more

Books

Big Book of Tractors (John Deere), Heather Alexander (DK Publishing, 2007)

The Usborne Book of Big Machines (Usborne Publishing Ltd, 2008)

Websites

www.bigfoot4x4.co.uk/thehistory.asp

www.jcbexplore.com

Index